JOURNAL

Peter Pauper Press, Inc.
WHITE PLAINS, NEW YORK

PETER PAUPER PRESS
Fine Books and Gifts Since 1928

Our Company

In 1928, at the age of twenty-two, Peter Beilenson began printing books on a small press in the basement of his parents' home in Larchmont, New York. Peter—and later his wife, Edna—sought to create fine books that sold at "prices even a pauper could afford."

Today, still family owned and operated, Peter Pauper Press continues to honor our founders' legacy—and our customers' expectations—of beauty, quality, and value.

The original version of the sumptuous jeweled binding for the *Rubáiyat of Omar Kkayyám*, created in 1911 by Francis Sangorski, went down on the *Titanic*. A subsequent recreation of the design by Stanley Bray was destroyed by a direct hit during the London Blitz. Some of the jewels were salvaged, however, and the undaunted Bray recreated the binding a second time in 1982 when he was 82. The design, reproduced on this journal cover, became known as *The Great Omar III*.

Copyright © 2013
Peter Pauper Press, Inc.
202 Mamaroneck Avenue
White Plains, NY 10601
All rights reserved
ISBN 978-1-4413-1221-1
Printed in China
14 13 12 11

Visit us at www.peterpauper.com